Work Book

Copyright (c) 2020 by Anthony Gitch - Excel Hypnosis

All rights reserved.

Published in the United States by Excel Hypnosis.

ISBN: 978-1-7354557-2-3

Printed in the United States of America.

Anthony Gitch, BCH, CI
Excel Hypnosis
901 Boren Ave, #1300
Seattle, WA 98104
206-549-1108
www.excelhypnosis.com

Table of Contents

Introduction 1

Your Calibration 2

Your Gratitude List 4

Your Beliefs 23

Your Truths 32

Your Mind 39

Your Energy System 43

Surrender and Acceptance 45

Faster EFT for You 50

Boundary Creation and Sharing 53

Basic Empowerment Questions 54

I Have A Problem 57

Finish 62

Recommend Reading 63

Introduction

Please enjoy this companion workbook for The Art of Self Destruction. For the most part, I follow with the content of the book and provide a deeper explanation for some of the existing activities and have provided many new activities here.

These activities are intended to be easy to follow but will provide you with new tools with which to exercise a greater variety of choice in your daily life. By having more choices, you will be more able to recognize the opportunities that exist all around you.

Visit the resource center at excelhypnosis.com/resources and watch the videos on how to perform the tapping and breathing plus more.

Your Calibration

What do I mean by calibration? I'm talking about a way to measure your success, feelings, pain levels, and more. Let's say, for example, you are working on being angry at work, and you want to feel better when things get stressful. How are you going to know if you are doing any better if you don't know where the starting line is?

Keep track of how many times per day you are getting frustrated or stressed. Then, as you begin to us the Control Valve technique you are about learn, notice how the number goes down and that you experience less time frustrated and more time being productive and achieving what you set out to do. The faster EFT technique is also fantastic for immediate recalibration from an unhelpful state to one of success and motivation.

Calibration of your feelings and pain is easy because you simply rate it from 0 – 10 with 0 being no feeling or no pain and 10 being the most extreme end of the feeling or intense pain.

Now you will lower the level of intensity from the current unhelpful sate by using your breath.

Yes, your breath is the foundation of your current state of mind. When you control the breath, you control everything else, including your emotional and physical responses.

Here is how it works, from the bottom to the top.

- Performance – action through flow or stagnation, fear or lack of confidence
- State of mind – ego state, archetype, or the part in control of the executive function
- Physiology – the condition of your body, pain level, hunger, or lack of sleep
- Breath – the foundational block that supports and is able to affect the other three

Level 1 is the main foundation; it holds up everything else. Level 1 is your breath. Level 2 is your physiology. This means making sure you're well-nourished each day and that you are taking care of yourself by getting enough exercise and sleep. Level two can be changed by how you breath. Your breath and physiology regulate your state of mind, which is level 3. Your state of mind determines how you are viewing the world, or rather, which archetype of ego sate has control. That brings us to level 4—your performance state. This is when you are performing at your best. You are relaxed and enjoying the flow of ideas and the exchange of

The Easiest Breath Empowerment Tool I Can Share
Is the Tried and True 7 – 11 Breathing

- First, when you inhale, your shoulders should not move. Your belly should expand but not your chest. I want you to breath into your belly and let the air push it out.
- Now, exhale very slowly to the count of 11. You exhale for a longer count to make sure you push your belly all the way back to your spine.
- It's simple. As you breath in through your nose, you will count, one-one thousand, two-one thousand, and so on, until you reach seven-one thousand. Then, without holding it, begin releasing your breath, slowly exhaling and counting to eleven-one thousand.

When you begin this exercise, rate your level of stress from 0 – 10.

1. I currently feel____. From 0 - 10 I am a currently at a _____ (I currently feel angry, sad, frustrated, overwhelmed. From 0 – 10, I am a currently at an 8).

2. The _____ I was feeling is lowered to a (0 - 10) _____(the anger, sadness, frustration, stress I was feeling is lowered to a (0 - 10).

Use the breathing tool and calibration tool and keep track of your success.

Your Gratitude List

I try my best not to assume anything, so I am going to give a bit of breakdown of what a gratitude list is, and why I think it is important to have one.

It is a way to begin to train your unconscious to form new neural connections that recognize the good in things or the positive aspects of situations. It is how we consciously begin to take control and force our negative thinking process out of the picture. And it is so easy because it only takes 10 minutes of your time. The trick of this is like the trick to everything—you have to do it.

There have been hundreds of research projects done around the world on the benefits of practicing gratitude. Here are just a few.

- Makes you happier
- Increases psychological well-being
- Enhances your positive emotions
- Increases your self-esteem
- Keeps suicidal thoughts and attempts at bay
- Improves your romantic relationships
- Improves your friendships
- Strengthens family relationships in times of stress
- Makes you more optimistic
- Makes you more giving
- Enhances optimism
- Reduces depressive symptoms
- Improves your sleep
- Improves your overall physical health
- Helps people recover from substance abuse
- Facilitates the recovery of depression

I am going to supply you with 30-days-worth of space to write down each day what you are grateful for. It can be as insignificant as the fact you have friends and clothing, to even being grateful that you have a beautiful smile.

Work Book

My 30-day gratitude list

Example:

Day 1 – Today I am grateful for *my friends and family being safe and healthy.*

Today I am grateful for *the fact I was able to get out of bed on time.*

Today I am grateful *knowing that I have a roof over my head.*

Today I am grateful for *my blue eyes.*

Today I am grateful for *my job.*

Today I am grateful for *my ability to look for work on the internet.*

Today I am grateful for *clean laundry.*

Today I am grateful for *a loving, understanding partner.*

Today I am grateful for *my kids.*

Today I am grateful for *the sunshine.*

Day 1 –

Today I am grateful for _____

Today I am grateful for _____

Today I am grateful for _____

Today I am grateful for _____

Today I am grateful for _____

Today I am grateful for _____

Today I am grateful for _____

Today I am grateful for _____

Today I am grateful for _____

Today I am grateful for _____

Day 2 –

Today I am grateful for _____

Today I am grateful for _____

Today I am grateful for _____

Today I am grateful for _____

Today I am grateful for _____

Today I am grateful for _____

Today I am grateful for _____

Today I am grateful for _____

Today I am grateful for _____

Today I am grateful for _____

Day 3 –

Today I am grateful for _____

Today I am grateful for _____

Today I am grateful for _____

Today I am grateful for _____

Today I am grateful for _____

Today I am grateful for _____

Today I am grateful for _____

Today I am grateful for _____

Today I am grateful for _____

Today I am grateful for _____

Day 4 –

Today I am grateful for _____

Today I am grateful for _____

Today I am grateful for _____

Today I am grateful for _____

Today I am grateful for _____

Today I am grateful for _____

Today I am grateful for _____

Today I am grateful for _____

Today I am grateful for _____

Today I am grateful for _____

Day 5 –

Today I am grateful for _____

Today I am grateful for _____

Today I am grateful for _____

Today I am grateful for _____

Today I am grateful for _____

Today I am grateful for _____

Today I am grateful for _____

Today I am grateful for _____

Today I am grateful for _____

Today I am grateful for _____

Day 6 –

Today I am grateful for _____

Today I am grateful for _____

Today I am grateful for _____

Today I am grateful for _____

Today I am grateful for _____

Today I am grateful for _____

Today I am grateful for _____

Today I am grateful for _____

Today I am grateful for _____

Today I am grateful for _____

Day 7 –

Today I am grateful for _____

Today I am grateful for _____

Today I am grateful for _____

Today I am grateful for _____

Today I am grateful for _____

Today I am grateful for _____

Today I am grateful for _____

Today I am grateful for _____

Today I am grateful for _____

Today I am grateful for _____

Day 8 –

Today I am grateful for _____

Today I am grateful for _____

Today I am grateful for _____

Today I am grateful for _____

Today I am grateful for _____

Today I am grateful for _____

Today I am grateful for _____

Today I am grateful for _____

Today I am grateful for _____

Today I am grateful for _____

Day 9 –

Today I am grateful for _____

Today I am grateful for _____

Today I am grateful for _____

Today I am grateful for _____

Today I am grateful for _____

Today I am grateful for _____

Today I am grateful for _____

Today I am grateful for _____

Today I am grateful for _____

Today I am grateful for _____

Day 10 –

Today I am grateful for _____

Today I am grateful for _____

Today I am grateful for _____

Today I am grateful for _____

Today I am grateful for _____

Work Book

Today I am grateful for _____

Today I am grateful for _____

Today I am grateful for _____

Today I am grateful for _____

Today I am grateful for _____

Day 11 –

Today I am grateful for _____

Today I am grateful for _____

Today I am grateful for _____

Today I am grateful for _____

Today I am grateful for _____

Today I am grateful for _____

Today I am grateful for _____

Today I am grateful for _____

Today I am grateful for _____

Today I am grateful for _____

Day 12 –

Today I am grateful for _____

Today I am grateful for _____

Today I am grateful for _____

Today I am grateful for _____

Today I am grateful for _____

Today I am grateful for _____

Today I am grateful for _____

Today I am grateful for _____

Today I am grateful for _____

Today I am grateful for _____

Day 13 –

Today I am grateful for _____

Today I am grateful for _____

Today I am grateful for _____

Today I am grateful for _____

Today I am grateful for _____

Today I am grateful for _____

Today I am grateful for _____

Today I am grateful for _____

Today I am grateful for _____

Today I am grateful for _____

Day 14 –

Today I am grateful for _____

Today I am grateful for _____

Today I am grateful for _____

Today I am grateful for _____

Today I am grateful for _____

Today I am grateful for _____

Today I am grateful for _____

Today I am grateful for _____

Today I am grateful for _____

Today I am grateful for _____

Day 15 –

Today I am grateful for _____

Today I am grateful for _____

Today I am grateful for _____

Today I am grateful for _____

Today I am grateful for _____

Today I am grateful for _____

Today I am grateful for _____

Today I am grateful for _____

Today I am grateful for _____

Today I am grateful for _____

Day 16 –

Today I am grateful for _____

Today I am grateful for _____

Today I am grateful for _____

Today I am grateful for _____

Today I am grateful for _____

Today I am grateful for _____

Today I am grateful for _____

Today I am grateful for _____

Today I am grateful for _____

Today I am grateful for _____

Day 17 –

Today I am grateful for _____

Today I am grateful for _____

Today I am grateful for _____

Today I am grateful for _____

Today I am grateful for _____

Today I am grateful for _____

Today I am grateful for _____

Today I am grateful for _____

Today I am grateful for _____

Today I am grateful for _____

Day 18 –

Today I am grateful for _____

Today I am grateful for _____

Today I am grateful for _____

Today I am grateful for _____

Today I am grateful for _____

Today I am grateful for _____

Today I am grateful for _____

Today I am grateful for _____

Today I am grateful for _____

Today I am grateful for _____

Day 19 –

Today I am grateful for _____

Today I am grateful for _____

Today I am grateful for _____

Today I am grateful for _____

Today I am grateful for _____

Today I am grateful for _____

Today I am grateful for _____

Today I am grateful for _____

Today I am grateful for _____

Today I am grateful for _____

Day 20 –

Today I am grateful for _____

Today I am grateful for _____

Today I am grateful for _____

Today I am grateful for _____

Today I am grateful for _____

Today I am grateful for _____

Today I am grateful for _____

Today I am grateful for _____

Today I am grateful for _____

Today I am grateful for _____

Day 21 –

Today I am grateful for _____

Today I am grateful for _____

Today I am grateful for _____

Today I am grateful for _____

Today I am grateful for _____

Today I am grateful for _____

Today I am grateful for _____

Today I am grateful for _____

Today I am grateful for _____

Today I am grateful for _____

Day 22 –

Today I am grateful for _____

Today I am grateful for _____

Today I am grateful for _____

Today I am grateful for _____

Today I am grateful for _____

Today I am grateful for _____

Today I am grateful for _____

Today I am grateful for _____

Today I am grateful for _____

Today I am grateful for _____

Day 23 –

Today I am grateful for _____

Today I am grateful for _____

Today I am grateful for _____

Today I am grateful for _____

Today I am grateful for _____

Today I am grateful for _____

Today I am grateful for _____

Today I am grateful for _____

Today I am grateful for _____

Today I am grateful for _____

Day 24 –

Today I am grateful for _____

Today I am grateful for _____

Today I am grateful for _____

Today I am grateful for _____

Today I am grateful for _____

Today I am grateful for _____

Today I am grateful for _____

Today I am grateful for _____

Today I am grateful for _____

Today I am grateful for _____

Day 25 –

Today I am grateful for _____

Today I am grateful for _____

Today I am grateful for _____

Today I am grateful for _____

Today I am grateful for _____

Today I am grateful for _____

Today I am grateful for _____

Today I am grateful for _____

Today I am grateful for _____

Today I am grateful for _____

Day 26 –

Today I am grateful for _____

Today I am grateful for _____

Today I am grateful for _____

Today I am grateful for _____

Today I am grateful for _____

Today I am grateful for _____

Today I am grateful for _____

Today I am grateful for _____

Today I am grateful for _____

Today I am grateful for _____

Day 27 –

Today I am grateful for _____

Today I am grateful for _____

Today I am grateful for _____

Today I am grateful for _____

Today I am grateful for _____

Today I am grateful for _____

Today I am grateful for _____

Today I am grateful for _____

Today I am grateful for _____

Today I am grateful for _____

Day 28 –

Today I am grateful for _____

Today I am grateful for _____

Today I am grateful for _____

Today I am grateful for _____

Today I am grateful for _____

Today I am grateful for _____

Today I am grateful for _____

Today I am grateful for _____

Today I am grateful for _____

Today I am grateful for _____

Day 29 –

Today I am grateful for _____

Today I am grateful for _____

Today I am grateful for _____

Today I am grateful for _____

Today I am grateful for _____

Today I am grateful for _____

Today I am grateful for _____

Today I am grateful for _____

Today I am grateful for _____

Today I am grateful for _____

Day 30 –

Today I am grateful for _____

Today I am grateful for _____

Today I am grateful for _____

Today I am grateful for _____

Today I am grateful for _____

Today I am grateful for _____

Today I am grateful for _____

Today I am grateful for _____

Today I am grateful for _____

Today I am grateful for _____

Your Beliefs

As you learned in the book, it was primarily my beliefs that caused me so much pain and unhappiness. Just as I did in the book, it is time to review your beliefs and determine if they are serving your highest good or are some of them keeping you where you don't want to be?

I want to you write down 3 of your beliefs that keep you from moving forward, for example: if you hate your job but you don't leave it because of you're are afraid you won't get another job. That is a belief.

Here is how to determine what some of your limiting beliefs are. If you start the sentence with:

I am not able to _____.

I am not able to finish school because it's too expensive.

If it wasn't for _____.

If it wasn't for my boss not liking me, I would have gotten a raise.

I can't because _____.

I can't apply for that position because I don't have the education requirements.

They won't let me _____.

They won't let me play on their team because I am a gay person.

I don't have _____.

I don't have the same opportunities as everyone else to get a good job.

Any time you start off with an explanation of why you can't, then you know that it is something to take through this process.

First you need to write down your limiting beliefs. That way at the end of 90, days you can review and see how far you have come to changing the way you think and believe about you and your ability to change and be successful.

Now, remember, a limiting belief can be anything; a thought or even thing that you feel is interfering with where you want to be, your happiness, or your level of success.

Belief: I can't apply for that position because I don't have the educational requirements.

Belief 1: _____

_____

_____

_____

Belief 2: _____

_____

_____

_____

Belief 3: _____

_____

_____

_____

Now that you have your limiting belief down on paper, it is time to look at the reality of them. Do those beliefs actually hold water? You will take each of your beliefs and put them through the reality checker to know if they are truly what is holding you back.

This activity will determine once and for all if the limiting belief is true or false. I already know that 99% of peoples' limiting believes are false, so I don't want more of my own proof. I want you to prove how it is true. Here's the deal, if you can't prove it's true then you are going to set yourself free from it forever, right here and now.

1. Is the limiting belief true?

1. You will need to provide at least 3 examples of how the limiting belief is true. These examples cannot be made up, they have to be verifiable with facts, not feelings.

Belief: I can't apply for that position because I don't have the educational requirements. *Truth 1: The post indicates they prefer someone with a degree. Truth 2: I don't have a degree. Truth 3: Everyone else in that position has a degree.*

— Please pay attention here. All three of the above "truths" are BS. None of them hold water as truths, and here is why.

Truth 1: The ad only PREFERS someone with a degree. I know from personal experience that even when they require a degree, it is not always necessary. My brother and I have both held positions that required degrees, and neither one of us have a degree in anything, but we know how to prove ourselves and demonstrate our abilities to adapt and pick up new skills with ease.

Truth 2: If you need a degree to prove to yourself that you are worthy of the things you want, then you better do what is necessary to make that happen, OR accept that you are perfectly able to do what you need to do without one. Refer back to the first answer to understand why this believe is not a valid truth.

Truth 3: How do you know everyone else in that position has one? Do you know everyone else in that position?

Belief 1: _____

_____

_____

_____

Belief 2: _____

_____

_____

_____

Belief 3: _____

_____

_____

_____

2. What needs to change in order to change the limiting belief?

Belief: I can't apply for that position because I don't have the educational requirements.

— I need to go back to school in order to get my degree. The company needs to lower the educational requirements for this position. I need to have more money so I can go back to school and get my degree.

Belief 1: _____

_____

_____

_____

Belief 2: _____

_____

_____

_____

Belief 3: _____

_____

_____

_____

3. What are the benefits of having this limiting belief?

Belief: I can't apply for that position because I don't have the educational requirements.

— *I can't think of any benefits for the limiting belief other than it gives me an excuse for not getting ahead, and it makes it easier to say it's not my fault.*

Belief 1: _____

_____

_____

_____

Belief 2: _____

_____

_____

_____

Belief 3: _____

_____

_____

_____

4. What are the benefits of changing this limiting belief?

Belief: I can't apply for that position because I don't have the educational requirements.

— *If I change it, I am free to explore greater opportunities for advancement. If I change it, then I take pressure off myself to go back to school when I don't want to go back to school. I will feel better about me. I will feel empowered to move forward based on my abilities, not on my education.*

Belief 1: _____

_____

_____

_____

Belief 2: _____

_____

_____

_____

Belief 3: _____

_____

_____

_____

5. How will you feel without the limiting belief?

Belief: I can't apply for that position because I don't have the educational requirements.

— *I will feel better inside about me. I won't feel like I am less than anyone else anymore. I will feel empowered to apply for any job I want based on what I have to offer.*

Belief 1: _____

_____

_____

_____

Belief 2: _____

_____

_____

_____

Belief 3: _____

_____

_____

_____

6. What needs to change about you in order to change the limiting belief?

Belief: I can't apply for that position because I don't have the educational requirements.

— I need to change the way I feel about the importance of a degree. I need to recognize what my abilities are and what I have to offer outside the educational structure of things. I need to change the way I was taught to think about higher education and what it means to success.

Belief 1: _____

_____

_____

_____

Belief 2: _____

_____

_____

Belief 3: _____

_____

_____

_____

Now take each of these beliefs and write the truth about it. Where have you been fooling yourself? Recreate the belief with a new positive twist.

Belief: I can't apply for that position because I don't have the educational requirements.

— I have been thinking all this time that my education was holding me back when it was not in my way. The only thing in my way was my belief that my education is what defines my abilities and not believing that my actual contributions count as much, if not more, than the time spent in a classroom.

— My new belief is that I can apply for any position that I feel I have either the educational OR applied skills that qualify me for it. My education will no longer be a barrier to my success.

Belief 1: _____

_____

_____

_____

Belief 2: _____

_____

_____

_____

Belief 3: _____

_____

_____

_____

Some limiting beliefs will turn out to be true. That sucks! But here is the positive thing about it—by taking the belief through this process, you will be able to recognize where you need to change something in order to turn it into a learning opportunity. How will you make it a non-limiting belief?

Your Truths

In the book, starting on page 28, I talk about what I call the 5 Truths about you. This activity is all about recognizing how the 5 Truths are alive and well in your life.

Truth 1: You are not broken.

Write down 10 things that prove this is true about you. Especially write down those things that come natural to you but maybe not for others. Write down the first things that come to your mind.

1. _____

2. _____

3. _____

4. _____

5. _____

6. _____

7. _____

8._____

_____

9._____

_____

10._____

_____

Truth 2: You are the co-creator of all your experiences.

It's time to start recognizing how you are responsible for what you experience. I want you to write down 5 times that you have responded to a negative situation with awareness and the intent to not let the situation control your current neutral or positive state, this is called conscious co-creation.

5 times you were practicing awareness and conscious co-creation.

1._____

_____

2._____

_____

3._____

_____

4._____

_____

5._____

_____

Now you will record 5 times you simply reacted without thinking. Write down 5 times you were not consciously aware and instead just reacting.

6. _____

_____

7. _____

_____

8. _____

_____

9. _____

_____

10. _____

_____

Truth 3: You have the power to forgive. In this activity, you will write down 3 people or 3 experiences that you are holding resentments about or are still angry about.

Thing / person 1: _____

_____

Thing / person 2: _____

_____

Thing / person 3: _____

_____

Now answer each of these questions about your answers.

Did what happened or what they did diminish who I am?

Thing / person 1: _____

_____

Thing / person 2: _____

_____

Thing / person 3: _____

_____

How will I feel different when I forgive them?

Thing / person 1: _____

_____

Thing / person 2: _____

_____

Thing / person 3: _____

_____

How will forgiving what happened set me free?

Thing / person 1: _____

_____

Thing / person 2: _____

_____

Thing / person 3: _____

_____

What is the benefit for the other person if I continue to hold onto this old hurt?

Thing / person 1: _____

_____

Thing / person 2: _____

_____

Thing / person 3: _____

_____

Once you have been through this process, go back to the book and revise the hypnotic process of ongoing forgiveness.

Truth 4: You are always teaching.

This is a super powerful one, and as I mention in the book: this is a no brainer if you're a parent. Even if you are not a parent, you are constantly teaching. You are teaching the people you interact with at work how to treat you by maintaining your boundaries, sense of moral and ethics, and by your own actions.

This activity is another one where you begin to recognize how powerful moving through life consciously can be by propelling you into amazing opportunities.

I want you to write down 10 things you have done that have taught something to someone either intentionally or not. The unintentional teachings are those things or actions you took that demonstrated your high sense of morals, values, or kindness, or even demonstrated a sense of vulnerability where others may not have. Those moments are powerful teachers for the people around us, and we must not forget that.

Work Book

1. _____

   _____

2. _____

   _____

3. _____

   _____

4. _____

   _____

5. _____

   _____

6. _____

   _____

7. _____

   _____

8. _____

   _____

9. _____

   _____

10. _____

    _____

Truth 5: You have freewill and the right to choose.

Here's another fun activity if you recall in activity 1 when you wrote down and then destroyed your old limiting beliefs by answering the questions and recognizing what you could do to change the belief.

Write down a new version of each belief, applying freewill and your right to choose how you want the ending to be. This is again a way to activate the solution seeking mechanism in your brain, the unconscious mind.

Belief 1: _____

_____

_____

_____

Belief 2: _____

_____

_____

_____

Belief 3: _____

_____

_____

_____

Work Book

Your Mind

This exercise is intended to teach you how to train your mind, or rather—an aspect of the mind called the Reticular Activating System, or RAS.

You have experienced the tangible effects of the RAS. For example, right after you purchased your new car and the moment you drove it off the lot, you started seeing it everywhere. This is the power of the unconscious mind in action. It is a heat seeking missile for what it is programmed to find, but it uses none of your conscious awareness to do the work. This is what some call the Law of Attraction. You are going to train your unconscious mind to be continually scanning the outside world for what you want or a way in which to obtain it.

By training the unconscious mind to focus and look for what you want, you are assigning a super computer a task that it likes to do, solve equations or problems. Your unconscious mind will begin to look for opportunities behind the scenes to get what you want because it wants to solve the equation or the problem and because you are creating these questions with a positive intent and in the form of, "How will I?" Your mind starts to recognize more opportunities.

It is also important to include a time reference for each question by starting or ending the sentence with, today.

So how do you take advantage of your RAS? Easy, you train it by asking how you will achieve what it is that you want and then answering those questions. But what questions should you be asking?

Here is an example of the first stage, the foundation, if you will.

"How will I have a successful day at work today?" Or: "Today, how will I be successful at work?"

Or if you are having trouble with a co-worker, you could start with: "How will I get along with Mary at work today?"

The real training of the brain begins by how you answer the questions. You are not writing the answers down. You are simply answering them in your head. There are no tricks, no breathing, no tapping, just you asking yourself the right questions and then responding with the appropriate answer.

Realize that by asking the question, you are giving the unconscious what it wants, a problem to solve, and by setting it up as a positive, you are forcing both the conscious and unconscious mind to tune into the winning ways to make whatever it is happen. You are teaching your brain to play the "Glad Game", to always look for and find the positive solution to any given situation. If you don't know the reference, then watch the movie "Pollyanna" with Halley Mills, it is a classic.

With the example above, "Today, how will I get along with Mary at work?" my mind has a ton of options to go to; I can stay away from Mary today, or I can get along with Mary today by ignoring her heavy perfume. I can get along with Mary at work today by being nice to her and not participating when others make fun of her behind her back.

You will now create 5 questions that contain within them the positive things you want to achieve.

1. Today how will I : _____

_____

2. Today how will I : _____

_____

3. Today how will I : _____

_____

4. Today how will I : _____

_____

5. Today how will I : _____

_____

Answering the questions is another area where you need to focus on the positive approach and allow your unconscious to provide you with the answers. And remember, there's an infinite number of possibilities or unlimited potential when it comes to how you will accomplish your goals.

After a couple of weeks of using the above tool and allowing time for you unconscious to begin to create these new thought patterns, I want to you change up and expand on your questions.

From the examples above: As I have a successful day at work today, how will I get self-satisfaction for my great work?

As I get along better with Mary, my workflow improves, and I get noticed for my contributions, how will I go above and beyond today?

1. As I : _____

_____

2. As I : _____

_____

3. As I : _____

_____

4. As I : _____

_____

5. As I : _____

_____

Tape this to your bathroom mirror or someplace where you are exposed to them daily, and each time you read them, answer them with a solution based approach, and you will find that things will begin to turn out the way you want.

Okay, you remember your old limiting beliefs from earlier? Good, this is where you are going to use your new system of thought to create "How will I" and "As I" statements with the new positive beliefs you came up with earlier to replace the old, untrue beliefs.

Belief 1: _____

_____

_____

_____

Belief 2: _____

_____

_____

_____

Belief 3: _____

_____

_____

_____

Your Energy System

In the book, I talk about the four survival archetypes and the influence they have over our daily existence, even when they are operating in the background out of your awareness. In this activity, you are going to identify just how each of these archetypes are influencing you and your daily life.

The Child:

What are the characteristics you display when you are experiencing the light side of this archetype?

_____

_____

_____

What are the characteristics you display when you are experiencing the shadow side of this archetype?

_____

_____

_____

The Prostitute:

What are the characteristics you display when you are experiencing the light side of this archetype?

_____

_____

_____

What are the characteristics you display when you are experiencing the shadow side of this archetype?

_____

_____

_____

The Victim:

What are the characteristics you display when you are experiencing the light side of this archetype?
___

___

___

What are the characteristics you display when you are experiencing the shadow side of this archetype?
___

___

___

The Saboteur:

What are the characteristics you display when you are experiencing the light side of this archetype?
___

___

___

What are the characteristics you display when you are experiencing the shadow side of this archetype?
___

___

___

Surrender and Acceptance

Surrender is easier to experience than it is to explain. Sounds funny, I know, but for me; practicing it is easy, I just let things unfold as they unfold, and when I can assert my influence to ensure that things turn out the way I want them to, then I do that. If, on the other hand, I determine that a confrontation, that is not worth it, is about to ensue, then I stand still and let it pass. It is all about doing my best to remain conscious and aware of what is influencing my current state of affairs and calibrating my actions to those influences. As I say in the book, it is like a surfer riding a wave, he does not judge what the water beneath his board is doing, he simply adjusts what he has control over to ensure the best ride he can have.

This activity is designed to show you how judging others keeps you from experiencing surrender. It will use your ability to imagine what it is like to be someone else.

Write down 10 things you judge others doing as bad.

1._____

_____

2._____

_____

3._____

_____

4._____

_____

5._____

_____

6._____

_____

7._____

_____

8._____

_____

9._____

_____

10._____

_____

Now, I want you to write from the perspective of the person you are judging. Take on the whole persona of the person who engages in these things that you judge as bad. This is where you get to be an actor, because I want to you imagine what it is like to be that other person. I want you become them for this activity. Really get into their skin and experience the world through their eyes, ears, mind, and body. Write down from their perspective why these things are really okay for them. Write down why they believe what they are doing is right from their point of view. Leave your voice out of it, remember; you are them and this is their turn to speak.

1._____

_____

2._____

_____

3._____

_____

4. _____

_____

5. _____

_____

6. _____

_____

7. _____

_____

8. _____

_____

9. _____

_____

10. _____

_____

What has changed?

_____

_____

After completing this part of the activity, do you feel differently?

_____

_____

Are you able to appreciate the other perspective?

_____

_____

Will you allow yourself to no longer be affected by whatever it was?

_____

_____

What did this tell you about yourself?

_____

_____

Now it is time for you to write down what you will do in order to no longer let these things bother you. How will you surrender?

1._____

_____

2._____

_____

3._____

_____

4._____

_____

5._____

_____

6. _____

_____

7. _____

_____

8. _____

_____

9. _____

_____

10. _____

_____

Faster EFT for You

As I explained in the Basic EFT chapter of the book, starting on page 94, EFT is a great tool for taking back control of your mood. It is a way to immediately take the charge out of a negative or painful experience, and this time, as an added bonus, I am going to show you how to replace the negative emotion with something positive.

In the book, I explain basic EFT and the proven techniques as prescribed by the creator Gary Craig. Since he started teaching it in the mid-90s, EFT has taken on many new skins all with good results.

I am going to teach you the one I learned from a teacher I greatly respect, Mike Mandel. This is called Faster EFT, and all by itself; it is a great tool, but when you backfill the space you just emptied of those negative feelings with a positive one, you are creating a greater sense of empowerment and control.

So why is it called faster EFT? Because it is faster to do than the other tapping I taught you in the book. In this rendition, we will only focus on 4 spots and a wrist squeeze, and we will use the same spots for putting in good stuff where we took the bad out.

1. The third eye or right between the eyes (tap x 6)

2. Beside or next to the eye on the ridge of the orbital bone near the temple (tap x 6)

3. Under the pupil of the eye on the ridge of the orbital bone (tap x 6)

4. Just off center at the base of the collar bone (tap x 6)

5. Then end with a deep breath and squeezing the wrist

First, we calibrate. What is the intensity of the emotion you are feeling? Give it a number between 1 and 10.

I am feeling _____. If I had to give it a number between 1 and 10, it would be a _____.

Now, while holding whatever the negative thought is in your head, like craving a cigarette or feeling angry, begin tapping on each of the spots mentioned above and repeat these phrases:

1. Letting it go.

2. Just letting it all go.

3. I don't need it anymore.

4. Just let it all go.

5. Peace.

Now, calibrate yourself. Notice how much it went down? You will keep doing it until you reach a zero!

SIDE NOTE: IF you are not getting results, go to a different room. I know it sounds crazy, but sometimes that works. Don't ask me why, because I don't know, I only know what my experience has shown me. It could be the energy in the room or wiring in the wall, but when you move to a different room, you will often get different results. It can be interesting to find out where energies are different in your living space.

Once you are able to get it down to a zero, it is time to start to fill in the empty spaces with something positive so the backfilling begins.

Tap on each spot again, this time you will say what you want in place of what you had.

For example: at each spot, you can tap and say:

1. I feel good.

2. I am feeling so good.

3. I enjoy feeling good.

4. I am just feeling good.

5. Peace.

You could also say something like; I can handle this, or I've got this.

Then calibrate. That's right, I want you calibrate how good you feel, and you will continue the tapping with the positive statements until you reach an 8 or higher.

Bonus Tap!

Here is one more tapping tool. This is definitely my favorite. It is one I learned while attending and presenting at the world's largest hypnosis convention that is held every August in lovely Las Vegas, Nevada called HypnoThoughts Live.

I was attending a workshop, and this is what we did to kick off each day, and I have been using it since. I do this just before going in front of a crowd for a presentation or teaching.

First, you need to find the right spot. It is on the backside of your hand in the center of the groove between the bones of your ring finger and the little finger. (Check the online resources if you're having difficulty finding it.)

Once you have found the spot, you will begin. First, stand up tall and proud. Start tapping the spot and make empowering statements. Shout them out if you can, and if you can't then shout them out on the inside.

You will tap and say:

I feel amazing!

I am powerful.

I can learn anything I want!

I can change!

As you see, you can use any empowering statement to create the physical state. Play with this one and see how far it takes you on creating empowering states.

Boundary Creation and Sharing

I added this chapter because it is imperative that you learn proper boundary creation for both protective and containment boundaries. It is important because I want you to start to share your findings and growth with friends and family. Tell them what you are doing and why, but I want you to do so in a healthy way. You see; when you share your experience, strength and hope with others, you create inner strength. And as you share your good will with others, they will inevitably begin to ask questions about how you are doing this amazing work, which provides you the opportunity to teach what you have been doing, and that helps you to understand things at an even deeper level.

Here is the basic definition of protective and containment boundaries. I want you to understand them fully so you can share appropriately with people.

A protective boundary helps you to interact with people while feeling safe from them intruding inappropriately on your physical, emotional, intellectual, spiritual, or sexual space.

Then there is the containment boundary. This boundary helps you be appropriate in your relationship with others. Your containment boundaries keep you from becoming offensive or intruding on someone else's physical, emotional, intellectual, spiritual, or sexual space.

If you are constantly calling your friends on the phone and whining, blaming, and complaining about your life, then this will be good practice for you. It is not appropriate to go around vomiting your problems all over everyone else; and doing so is as gross as the analogy. It is okay to call a friend and have a venting session, but you need to always wrap it up with something positive, otherwise you become a black hole, sucking the enjoyment out of everything.

You must share what is working or as they say in the program: Share the message not the mess. This means to share your experience, strength, and hope so that others may be guided and inspired by what you are accomplishing and learn from your mistakes.

Anthony Gitch

Basic Empowerment Questions

1. How will I have a successful day today?

___

___

2. How will I maintain a great mood and share joy with others today?

___

___

3. How will I be of service to others today?

___

___

4. As I have a successful day, how will I help others have a good day?

___

___

5. As I overcome my limiting beliefs, how will I begin to get more from life today?

___

___

6. How will I begin to implement appropriate boundaries today?

___

___

7. How will I have a day filled with laugher and joy today?

_____

_____

8. How will I feel more self-confident today?

_____

_____

9. How will I create greater success at work for me today?

_____

_____

10. As I feel more confident in my work today, how will I help others do the same?

_____

_____

11. How will I be a better mother, father, brother, sister, son, daughter, husband, or wife today?

_____

_____

12. How will I grow today?

_____

_____

13. How will I leave a good impression on my boss today?

_____

_____

14. How will I reach my goals today?

_____

_____

15. As I reach my goals, how will I celebrate my victories?

_____

_____

Work Book

I Have A Problem

How many times have you said that or heard that? Too many to count, I know. You are going to take one of those problems and take it through these questions so you can find out more about the issue and why you may be holding onto it.

You may find that there is an unconscious benefit to this problem, and if that is the case, you will need to reevaluate your approach to solving the issue. When you find that on an unconscious level a problem you have appears to benefit you, this is called "Secondary gain," and it needs to be rooted out and resolved in order to fully move forward.

Secondary gain generally presents more when it comes to physical issues like fibromyalgia, back pain, or other physical pain, but it can show up with emotional issues as well.

So, for this activity, write down one of your problems, take it through the list of questions, and answer each one honestly.

As an example, I will use "chronic pain" as my problem.

1. What is the problem? _____

1. *What is the problem? I have chronic pain.*

2. What have I done in the past to fix this?

_____

_____

2. *What have I done in the past to fix this? Medication, yoga, acupuncture, meditation, relaxation*

3. What has worked and what has not worked?

_____

_____

3. *What has worked and what has not worked?* <u>Relaxation, meditation and medication worked — acupuncture and yoga did not work.</u>

4. What has worked and how did it work?

_____

_____

4. *What has worked and how did it work?* <u>Relaxation, meditation, and medication. They all work by calming me down and helping me be less anxious. I was even able to go back to work at a job I really liked until Covid came along.</u>

5. How bad does it feel right now? (0 - 10)

_____

_____

5. How bad does it feel right now? (0 - 10) - 8

6. What has made it worse?

_____

_____

6. *What has made it worse?* <u>Stress from Covid and isolation, not working, stress about money, and fear of getting sick. Not being able to provide for my family. The stress it is putting on my marriage.</u>

7. What will happen when you fix this? (What will change in your life?)

_____

_____

7. *What will happen when you fix this? (What will change in your life?)* <u>If I fix this, I can be me again. I can play with my kids and have a fun time with my friends and family. When I fix this, I will have to go work again.</u>

8. What will happen if you don't fix this?

_____

_____

8. *What will happen if you don't fix this?* *If I don't fix this, I will be more isolated than I am right now. I won't be able play with my kids or dog. I won't be able to have the life I really want to have.*

9. What does the problem permit you to do?

_____

_____

9. *What does the problem permit you to do?* *This problem allows me to be on Social Security, so I don't have to work 40 hours a week. This problem gives me the okay to ask my friends and family members for favors to help me out with cleaning, shopping, and taking care of my needs. This problem permits me to stay at home on the couch and not do anything productive if I don't feel like it. This problem allows me to see my family and friends more often.*

10. What does the problem prevent you from doing?

_____

_____

10. *What does the problem prevent you from doing?* *This problem prevents me from having a full-time job. This problem prevents me from doing things with my friends and family. This problem prevents me from feeling good about myself. This problem prevents me from reaching my goals and dreams.*

11. What does the problem permit you NOT to do?

_____

_____

11. *What does the problem permit you NOT to do?* *This problem permits me to not get a full-time job so I can spend more time with my grandkids. It permits me to not be able to take care of myself, so my son and his family need to come over more often and help me. It permits me to not be successful at attaining my goals.*

12. What does the problem prevent you from not doing?

_____

_____

12. *What does the problem prevent you from not doing?* *Nothing It supports me not doing anything.*

13. How do you know you even have a problem?

_____

_____

13. *How do you know you even have a problem?* *I know I have a problem because my back hurts all the time.*

14. How will you know you no longer have this problem?

_____

_____

14. *How will you know you no longer have this problem?* *When my back doesn't hurt all day.*

15. How ready are you to change this problem, form 0 - 10?

_____

_____

15. *How ready are you to change this problem, form 0 - 10?* *10*

16. Explain why you choose that number and not a lower one?

_____

_____

16. *Explain why you choose that number and not a lower one?* *10 because I want to feel better and I am ready to do what it will take to feel better now.*

How did you answer questions 9 and 11? These are areas you want to keep an eye on, and these are the areas you want to focus more detailed work on.

The client who answered the scenario told you a lot about their desire to work and their need to be cared for. They spoke of a fear of not seeing their friends and family as often if they get better. They spoke of a fear of losing out on Social Security if they got better. Don't judge! This is not a conscious behavior pattern. This is a survival pattern, one based in fear, and the person who does this is not aware they are doing it. That is why these questions are so valuable for you in determining how and where your responsibility resides in creating your problems, and then leading toward an appropriate solution.

Now that you have completed this, write down the things you can do right now that will change your experience of the problem. What is within your power and control in this moment that you can do to make this problem go away? Notice that the answer to this question may lead you to the conclusion that it is time to ask for help.

If you are at the top end of the scale and wanting to make a change, then it is the perfect time to seek out the appropriate professional to help guide you further. You have made the decision to change both consciously and unconsciously, so the process will be easy for you. Go out and find a fantastic coach, mentor, teacher, hypnotist, or counselor that you feel will best guide you on your new path to success.

Finish

I am grateful that you believed enough in yourself to take on these simple activities and new ways of thinking, feeling, and behaving.

Continue on your journey and remember; each day we are able to change the things about us that don't serve us.

It will serve you well to consider that mistakes will be made, and that is okay, but on this new journey, you take responsibility for your short comings and misdeeds, and sometimes that means eating crow. It is okay to admit when you are wrong. It shows wisdom when you demonstrate a willingness to be open to change.

Recommend Reading

Here is a short list of a few of my favorite books. I share this list with the clients I work with. Some of them are better than others but all are great to have in your library.

Robin Norwood

Women Who Love Too Much

Byron Katie:

Loving What Is

I Need Your Love, Is That True?

Dr. Richard K Nongard

The Seven Most Effective Ways Of Self Hypnosis

The Couples Treasure Chest.

Eckart Tolle

The Power Of Now

A New Earth.

Maxwell Maltz

Psycho Cybernetics

Pam Grout

E-Squard

Deepak Chopra

The Book Of Secrets

Quantum Healing

Carolyn Myss

Anatomy Of The Spirit

Energy Anatomy

Bruce Lipton, PhD

The Biology Of Belief

Pia Mellody

Facing Love Addiction

Calvin Banyan

The Secret Language of Feelings

www.ingramcontent.com/pod-product-compliance
Lightning Source LLC
Chambersburg PA
CBHW081253040426
42453CB00014B/2404